ALLOSAURUS

by Laura K. Murray

Consultant: Mathew J. Wedel, PhD
Western University of Health Sciences
Pomona, California

PEBBLE
a capstone imprint

Published by Pebble, an imprint of Capstone
1710 Roe Crest Drive, North Mankato, Minnesota 56003
capstonepub.com

Copyright © 2026 by Capstone. All rights reserved. No part of this publication may be reproduced in whole or in part, or stored in a retrieval system, or transmitted in any form or by any means, electronic, mechanical, photocopying, recording, or otherwise, without written permission of the publisher.

Library of Congress Cataloging-in-Publication Data is available on the Library of Congress website.

ISBN: 9798875226779 (hardcover)
ISBN: 9798875233982 (paperback)
ISBN: 9798875233999 (ebook PDF)

Summary: Describes Allosaurus, where it lived, what it ate, how it behaved, how it was discovered, and more.

Editorial Credits
Designer: Dina Her; Media Researcher: Jo Miller; Production Specialist: Tori Abraham

Image Credits
Capstone: Jon Hughes, cover, 1, 4, 5, 6, 8, 9, 11, 12, 15, 16, 17, 18, 19, 21; Getty Images: Ulrich Baumgarten, 27; Science Source: MARK GARLICK, 10, Francois Gohier, 23, Tom McHugh, 25; Shutterstock: Kues, background (throughout), racksuz, 13, Steve Bower, 28, Vladimir Bolokh, 20

Any additional websites and resources referenced in this book are not maintained, authorized, or sponsored by Capstone. All product and company names are trademarks™ or registered® trademarks of their respective holders.

Printed and bound in China. 006276

Table of Contents

Different Dinosaur 4

Where in the World 7

Allosaurus Bodies 10

What Allosaurus Ate 16

Life of Allosaurus 20

Discovering Allosaurus 22

Fast Facts 29

Glossary 30

Read More 31

Internet Sites 31

Index 32

About the Author 32

Words in **bold** are in the glossary.

Different Dinosaur

What huge dinosaur ran on two feet and had razor-sharp teeth? Allosaurus! Its name means "different reptile." The name came from the shape of its spine bones. They were a different shape from what scientists had seen before.

Allosaurus was the most common large **predator** of its time. It lived during the Late Jurassic Period. That was 152 to 145 million years ago.

Where in the World

Allosaurus lived in what is now North America and Europe. In the United States, it lived in Colorado, Montana, Oklahoma, Utah, and Wyoming. In Europe, scientists have found Allosaurus **fossils** in Portugal. Fossils found in Africa and other places may be Allosaurus too.

These places are far apart now. But Earth's land was different millions of years ago. It was one piece at the start of the Jurassic Period. By the time Allosaurus lived, the land had begun to split apart.

When Allosaurus lived, the land was warmer and wetter than it is today. Allosaurus roamed the flat land near rivers and streams. Shrubs, ferns, tall trees, and other plants grew there.

Turtles, lizards, and crocodiles lived in the area. **Mammals** there were small, like mice. Other dinosaurs included Apatosaurus and Stegosaurus.

Allosaurus Bodies

Allosaurus grew 30 to 40 feet (9 to 12 meters) in length. A big tail made up about half this length.

Allosaurus was up to 16 feet (4.9 m) tall. It stood on two powerful legs. It weighed 1.5 to 2 tons.

Scientists think some Allosaurus had feathers. The feathers may have grown in a line along its spine.

Allosaurus had a narrow snout. It had short horns above its eyes. The horns were made of bone. A bony ridge ran from the nose to the eyes.

The horns may have had different uses. They may have been used to show off to **mates**. They may have helped block the sun. They could have helped in fights too.

Allosaurus could open its jaws wide. It had 70 teeth. They were as sharp as razors. They curved backward. Each tooth was about 3 inches (7.6 centimeters) long. They snapped together to catch **prey**.

The teeth had ridges like a saw. This helped Allosaurus cut its food into bites. When Allosaurus lost a tooth, a new tooth grew in its place.

Did You Know?

Allosaurus teeth had points like steak knives.

What Allosaurus Ate

Allosaurus was a meat-eater. It ate smaller dinosaurs. Scientists think it ate big dinosaurs too. It may have eaten large, plant-eating dinosaurs that were young, old, or sick. These included Apatosaurus, Diplodocus, and Stegosaurus.

Allosaurus may have been a scavenger. Scavengers eat animals that are already dead or dying. This could explain how it ate larger dinosaurs. Allosaurus sometimes ate its own dead.

Scientists are not sure how Allosaurus hunted. They may have hunted alone. They may have hunted in packs. A group could work together to take down larger prey.

    Allosaurus could run about 20 miles (32.2 kilometers) per hour. It used its speed, size, teeth, and claws to catch its prey. Allosaurus may have eaten like a hawk. It pinned down its meal. It opened its jaws wide. Then it ripped off the meat.

Life of Allosaurus

Like other dinosaurs, Allosaurus hatched from an egg. As Allosaurus grew up, it could be injured in attacks by other dinosaurs. It could get sick. It could starve when food was hard to find.

Scientists study Allosaurus fossils. These fossils give clues about how the dinosaur lived, acted, and died. Life wasn't easy. Fossils show bite marks and injuries. Allosaurus bones were broken and healed.

Discovering Allosaurus

In 1877, scientist Othniel Charles Marsh named Allosaurus. Marsh was in a race with another scientist, Edward Drinker Cope. They tried to find the most fossils. Their race was called the Bone Wars.

In 1929, scientists began digging in a Utah **quarry**. It is part of an area called the Morrison Formation. People found many Allosaurus fossils there.

> **Did You Know?**
> Allosaurus is the state fossil of Utah.

Scientists dig at the Morrison Formation.

In 1991, scientists found an Allosaurus fossil in Shell, Wyoming. They named the skeleton Big Al. The Allosaurus had died near a riverbed. Its bones were covered by water and sand. It had been around 17 years old.

Scientists studied Big Al to learn about the dinosaur's life. Big Al had 19 bones affected by injury or disease. Soon, Big Al became famous. There was even a TV show about it.

There are different kinds of Allosaurus. Scientists do not agree on how many. Some Allosaurus have different body types. Their snouts may be longer or shorter. Their horns and skulls have different shapes. Scientists keep finding new information.

In 1996, scientists found another Allosaurus in Wyoming. They named it Big Al Two. It was one of the most complete Allosaurus skeletons ever found. It was about 25 feet (7.6 m) long.

Did You Know?

Scientists sculpted the missing bones of Big Al Two to make the full skeleton.

Big Al Two

In 2020, a new kind of Allosaurus was named. It was found in Utah in the early 1990s. The new Allosaurus was the oldest yet. It had a bony ridge above its eyes.

Today, scientists keep looking for clues about Allosaurus. They ask questions. They work to find the answers about these amazing Jurassic dinosaurs!

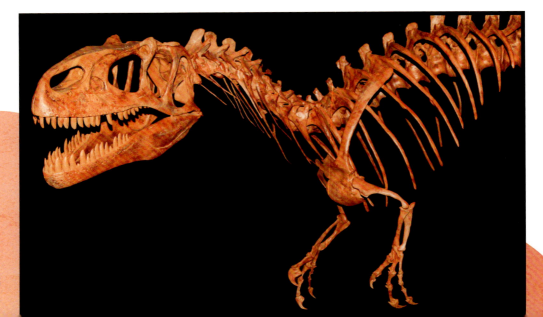

Fast Facts

Name: Allosaurus ("different reptile")

Lived: Late Jurassic Period
(about 152 to 145 million years ago)

Range: North America, Europe

Habitat: floodplains, river valleys

Food: other animals, including other dinosaurs; animal remains

Threats: no direct predators; injury or sickness

Discovered: 1877

Glossary

fossil (FAH-suhl)—the remains or traces of a living thing from many years ago

mammal (MAM-uhl)—a warm-blooded animal that has hair or fur; mammals usually give birth to live young

mate (MAYT)—a partner that joins with another to produce young

predator (PRED-uh-tur)—an animal that hunts other animals for food

prey (PRAY)—an animal that is hunted or killed by another animal for food

quarry (KWA-ree)—a big, deep pit made by humans

Read More

Finn, Peter. *Huge Allosaurus*. New York: Enslow Publishing, 2022.

Hulick, Kathryn. *Dinosaurs*. Minneapolis: Early Encyclopedias, 2023.

Sabelko, Rebecca. *Allosaurus*. Minneapolis: Bellwether Media, 2021.

Internet Sites

American Museum of Natural History: Allosaurus amnh.org/exhibitions/permanent/saurischian -dinosaurs/allosaurus

National Geographic Kids: Allosaurus kids.nationalgeographic.com/animals/prehistoric /facts/allosaurus

Natural History Museum: Allosaurus nhm.ac.uk/discover/dino-directory/allosaurus.html

Index

discovery, 7, 22, 24, 26, 28, 29

eggs, 20

feathers, 12

fossils, 7, 21, 22, 24

horns, 13, 26

legs, 11

mates, 13

name, 4, 22, 29

prey, 14, 16, 17, 18, 19, 29

size, 4, 10, 11

tail, 10

teeth, 4, 14, 15, 19

when it lived, 5, 7, 29

where it lived, 7, 29

About the Author

Laura K. Murray is the Minnesota-based author of more than 100 books for young readers. She loves learning from fellow readers and helping others find their reading superpowers! Visit LauraKMurray.com.